GRAPHIC SCIENCE

A REFRESHING LOOK AT

RENEWABLE ENERGY

WITH MAX AXIOM
SUPER SCIENTIST

by Katherine Krohn

illustrated by Cynthia Martin and Barbara Schulz

Consultant:

Ingrid Kelley

LEED AP, Project Manager

Energy Center of Wisconsin

Madison, Wisconsin

Capstone
Press

Mankato, Minnesota

Graphic Library is published by Capstone Press,
151 Good Counsel Drive, P.O. Box 669, Mankato, Minnesota 56002.
www.capstonepress.com

 Books published by Capstone Press are manufactured with paper
containing at least 10 percent post-consumer waste.

Library of Congress Cataloging-in-Publication Data
Krohn, Katherine E.
    A refreshing look at renewable energy with Max Axiom, super scientist / by Katherine
Krohn; illustrated by Cynthia Martin and Barbara Schulz.
    p. cm. — (Graphic library. Graphic science)
    Includes bibliographical references and index.
    Summary: "In graphic novel format, follows the adventures of Max Axiom as he
explores various sources of renewable energy" — Provided by publisher.
    ISBN 978-1-4296-3413-7 (library binding)
    ISBN 978-1-4296-3902-6 (softcover)
    1. Renewable energy sources — Juvenile literature. I. Martin, Cynthia, 1961- ill. II.
Schulz, Barbara (Barbara Jo), ill. III. Title. IV. Series.
TJ808.2.K76 2010
333.79'4 — dc22   2009001170

Designer
Alison Thiele

Cover Artist
Tod G. Smith

Cover Colorist
Krista Ward

Colorist
Matt Webb

Media Researcher
Wanda Winch

Editor
Christopher L. Harbo

Photo illustration credits: iStockphoto/Gord Horne, 25; Shutterstock/Dimyadi Hywit, 10

TABLE OF CONTENTS

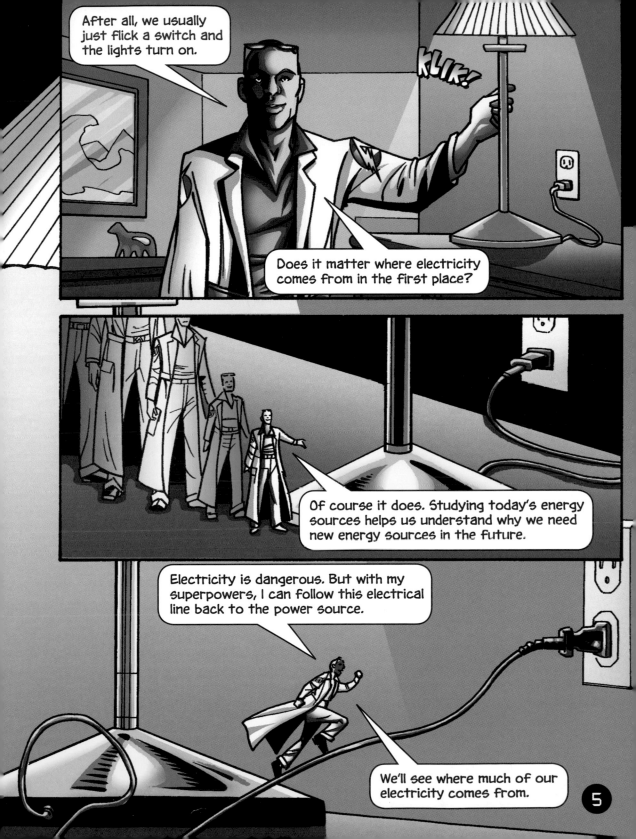

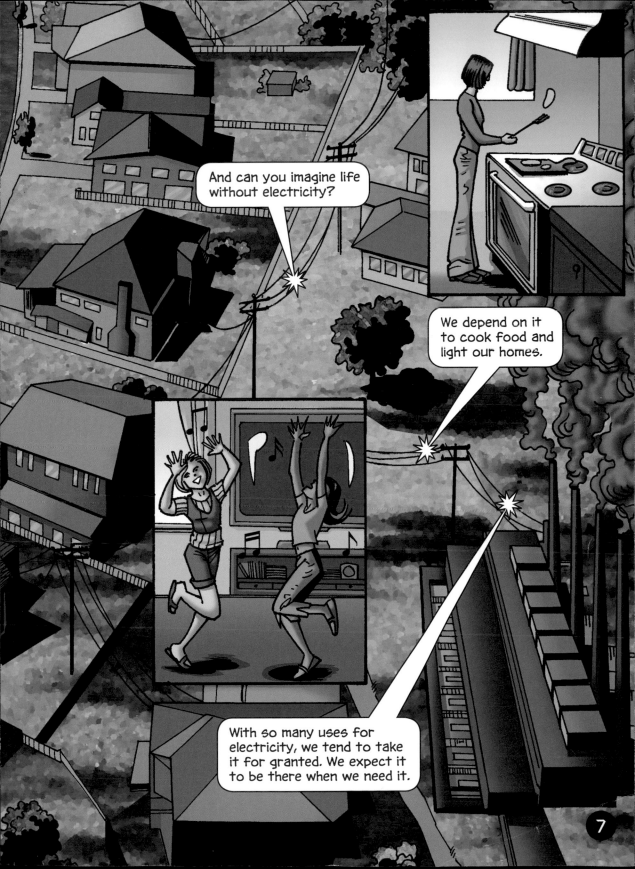

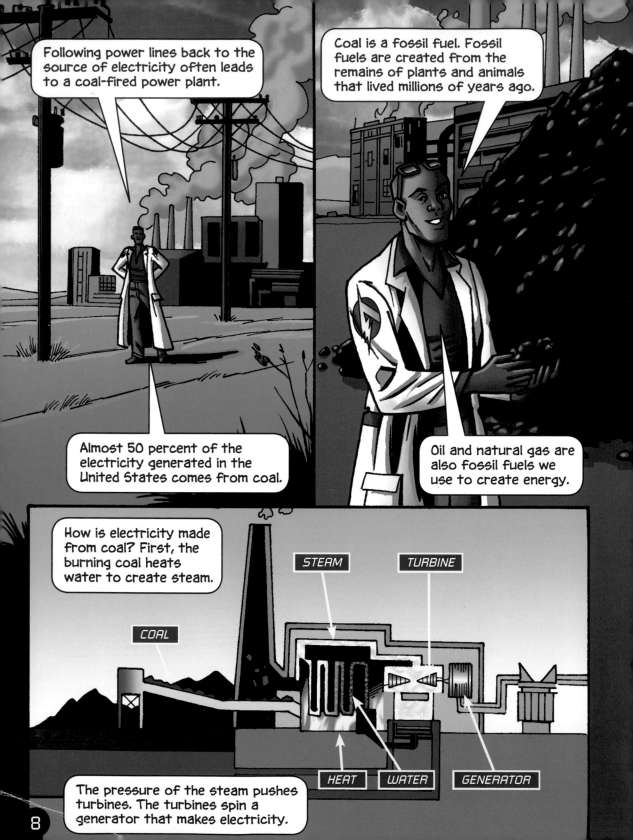

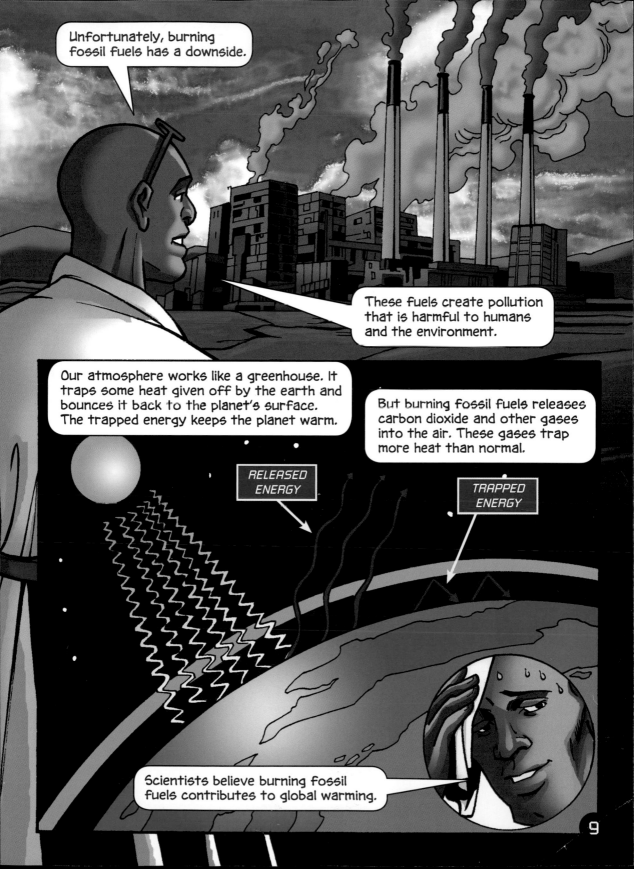

The limited supply of fossil fuels is another problem with this energy source.

Coal, oil, and natural gas are nonrenewable resources. That means someday we will run out of them.

COAL

OIL

NATURAL GAS

CLEAN COAL?

ACCESS GRANTED: MAX AXIOM

Researchers have developed ways to clean coal by removing pollutants before it is burned. But pollutants like carbon dioxide must be captured and stored to prevent them from being released into the air. Carbon storage technology is still experimental and expensive.

To confront issues like limited natural resources and global warming, people are turning to renewable energy sources.

Energy sources are found everywhere in nature. The sun shines, the wind blows, and crops grow. These energy sources are renewable.

They are all part of ongoing natural cycles. They create little or no pollution.

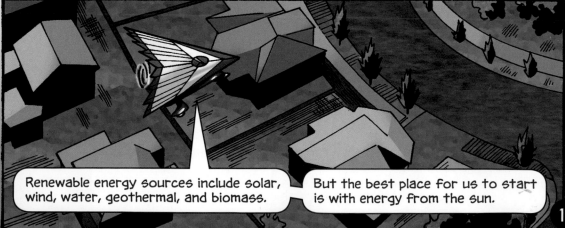

Renewable energy sources include solar, wind, water, geothermal, and biomass.

But the best place for us to start is with energy from the sun.

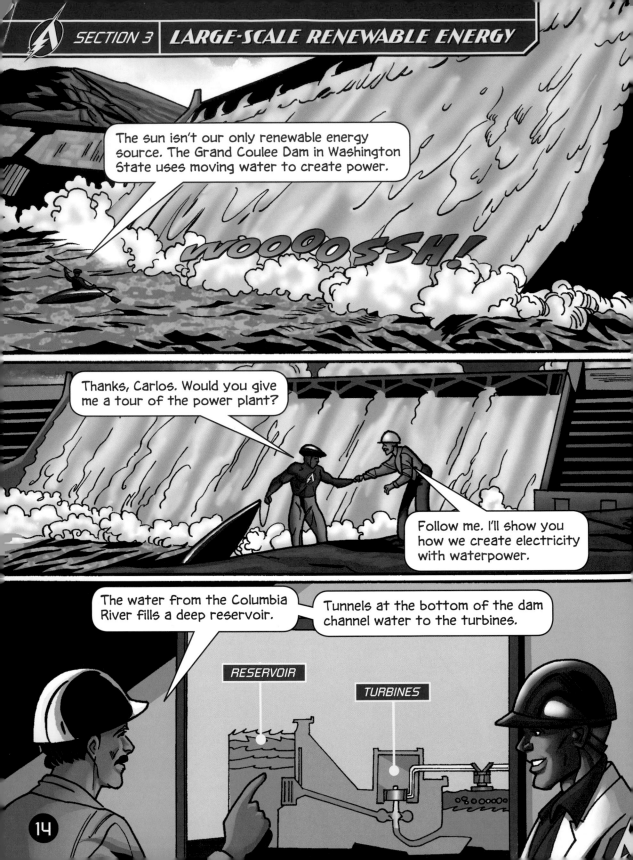

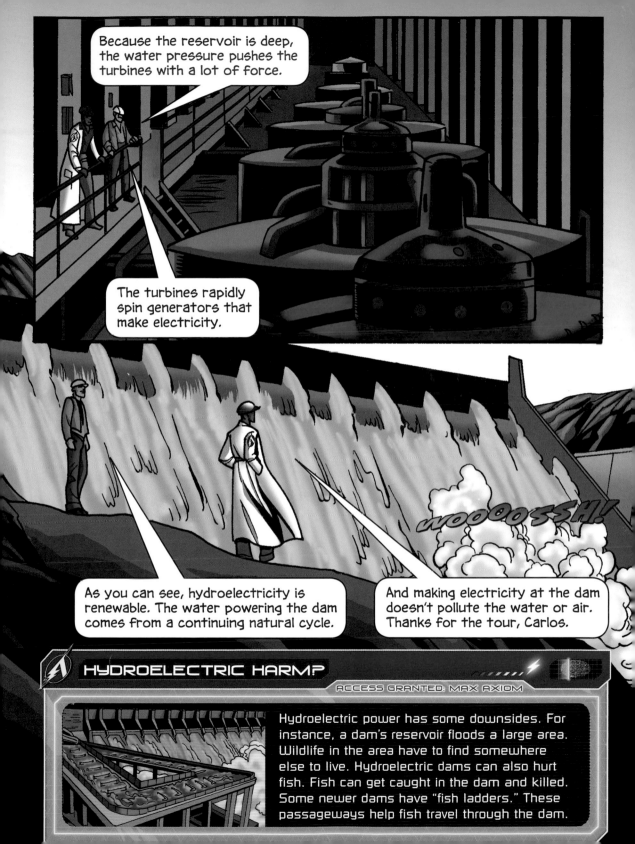

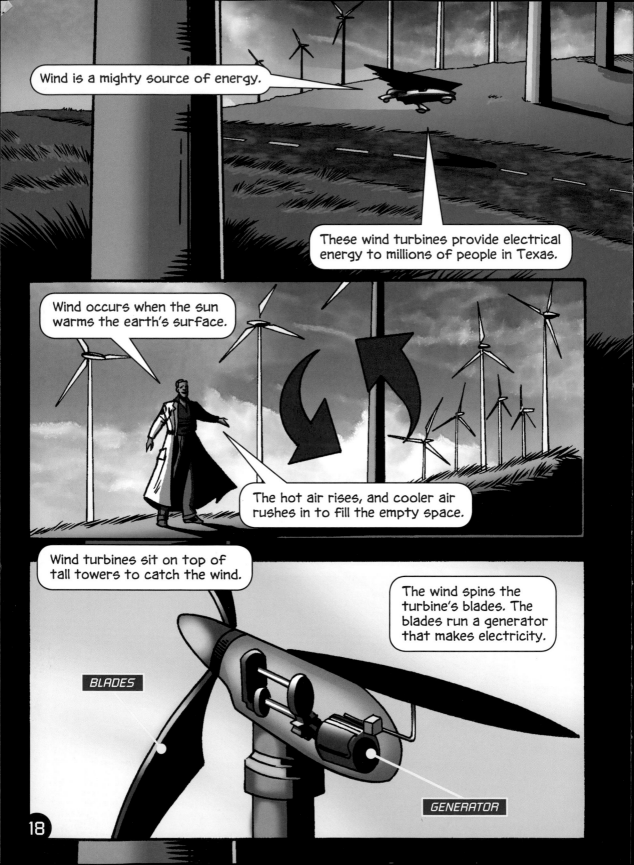

We've seen solar power used on a small scale. Now let's look at solar power on a large scale.

In California, the Mojave Desert has many solar power plants.

It's a perfect place to capture sunlight because the sun shines down regularly and it rarely rains.

⚡ POWER FROM SPACE

Scientists are working on new ways to use solar panels in space. The panels would change solar energy into a wavelength known as a microwave. These energy waves would be beamed to earth and changed into electricity.

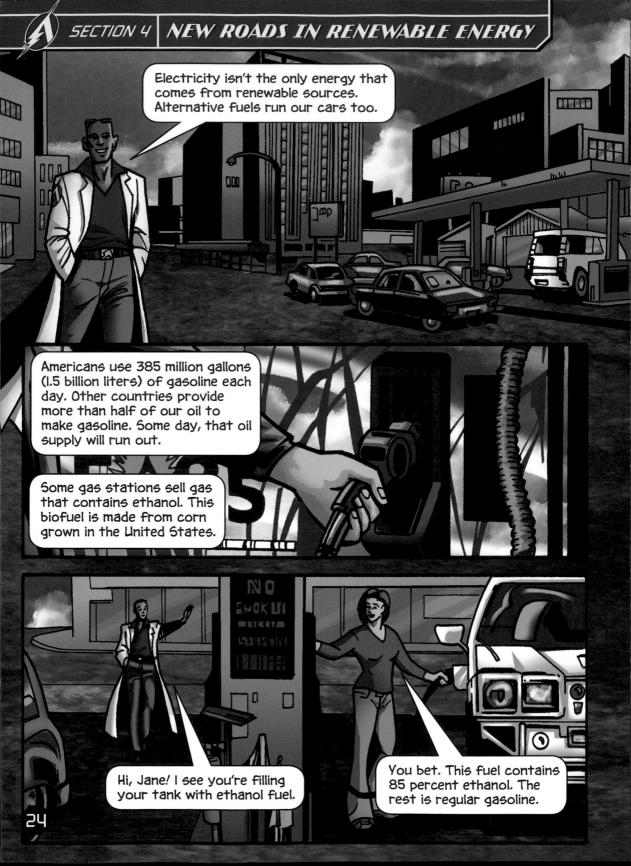

Electricity isn't the only energy that comes from renewable sources. Alternative fuels run our cars too.

Americans use 385 million gallons (1.5 billion liters) of gasoline each day. Other countries provide more than half of our oil to make gasoline. Some day, that oil supply will run out.

Some gas stations sell gas that contains ethanol. This biofuel is made from corn grown in the United States.

Hi, Jane! I see you're filling your tank with ethanol fuel.

You bet. This fuel contains 85 percent ethanol. The rest is regular gasoline.

As we've seen, renewable energy sources can be found in unusual places.

Believe it or not, this landfill is a good source of renewable energy too.

Plant and animal waste, such as food scraps, lawn clippings, and manure, are forms of biomass. Buried in landfills, this biomass releases methane gas.

When released into the atmosphere, methane acts as a greenhouse gas, which contributes to global warming.

METHANE DRILL

But methane from landfills can be burned like natural gas. It can power turbines that generate electricity.

If we use gases from landfills, we release less methane into our atmosphere.

27

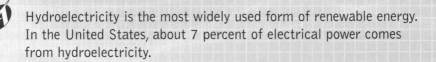

MORE ABOUT RENEWABLE ENERGY

Hydroelectricity is the most widely used form of renewable energy. In the United States, about 7 percent of electrical power comes from hydroelectricity.

Capturing energy from the sun is not a new idea. In the 1500s, artist and inventor Leonardo da Vinci sketched plans for using solar energy to heat water.

Only about 1 percent of the United States' electricity comes from wind power. Scientists estimate that by 2030, nearly 20 percent of U.S. energy will come from wind.

Researchers are working on putting solar farms on the ocean. But some scientists believe that solar panels on the ocean would block sunlight and upset the ocean's animal and plant life.

Almost all of Iceland's electricity comes from geothermal and hydroelectric energy sources. Most of Iceland's homes are heated with geothermal energy.

Scientists have found a way to make biofuel from algae. Algae is easy to grow and takes up less space than land crops like corn or soybeans.

In 1896, inventor Henry Ford designed his first car to run on 100 percent ethanol fuel.

A fuel cell is like a battery. It converts chemical energy into electricity. Today, fuel cells are an experimental source of power in some buildings. Automakers are developing cars that use hydrogen fuel cells. These cars use hydrogen fuel, instead of gasoline or diesel fuel, to run an electric motor.

 Used vegetable oil from fast food restaurants doesn't have to go to waste. It can be recycled to power cars. The vegetable oil is combined with ingredients such as lye and methanol to make biofuel. This "fast food fuel" works great — and it smells like french fries!

MORE ABOUT

SUPER SCIENTIST

Real name: Maxwell J. Axiom
Hometown: Seattle, Washington
Height: 6' 1"   **Weight:** 192 lbs
Eyes: Brown   **Hair:** None

Super capabilities: Super intelligence; able to shrink to the size of an atom; sunglasses give x-ray vision; lab coat allows for travel through time and space.

Origin: Since birth, Max Axiom seemed destined for greatness. His mother, a marine biologist, taught her son about the mysteries of the sea. His father, a nuclear physicist and volunteer park ranger, schooled Max on the wonders of earth and sky.

One day on a wilderness hike, a megacharged lightning bolt struck Max with blinding fury. When he awoke, Max discovered a newfound energy and set out to learn as much about science as possible. He traveled the globe earning degrees in every aspect of the field. Upon his return, he was ready to share his knowledge and new identity with the world. He had become Max Axiom, Super Scientist.

Glossary

biofuel (BYE-oh-fyoo-uhl) — a fuel made of, or produced from, plant material

biomass (BYE-oh-mass) — plant materials and animal waste used as a source of fuel

crust (KRUHST) — the thin outer layer of earth's surface

ethanol (ETH-uh-nal) — a biofuel made from crops such as corn and sugarcane

fossil fuels (FOSS-uhl FYOO-uhls) — natural fuels formed from the remains of plants and animals; coal, oil, and natural gas are fossil fuels.

generator (JEN-uh-ray-tur) — a machine that makes electricity by turning a magnet inside a coil of wire

geothermal (jee-oh-THUR-muhl) — relating to the intense heat inside the earth

hydraulic (hye-DRAW-lik) — having to do with a system powered by fluid forced through pipes or chambers

hydroelectricity (hye-droh-i-lek-TRISS-uh-tee) — a form of energy caused by flowing water

microwave (MYE-kroh-wave) — a wavelength in the electromagnetic spectrum

reservoir (REZ-ur-vwar) — a holding area for large amounts of water or steam

turbine (TUR-bine) — an engine powered by steam or gas

READ MORE

Jefferis, David. *Green Power: Eco-Energy without Pollution.* Science Frontiers. New York: Crabtree, 2006.

McLeish, Ewan. *Energy Crisis: A Look at the Way the World is Today.* Issues of the World. Mankato, Minn.: Stargazer Books, 2007.

Morgan, Sally. *From Windmills to Hydrogen Fuel Cells: Discovering Alternative Energy.* Chain Reactions. Chicago: Heinemann Library, 2007.

Saunders, Nigel. *Wind Power.* Energy for the Future and Global Warming. Pleasantville, N.Y.: Gareth Stevens, 2008.

Snedden, Robert. *Energy Alternatives.* Essential Energy. Chicago: Heinemann Library, 2006.

INTERNET SITES

FactHound offers a safe, fun way to find Internet sites related to this book. All sites on FactHound have been researched by our staff.

Here's all you do:

Visit *www.facthound.com*

FactHound will fetch the best sites for you!